MW01200279

ENDORSEMENTS FOR SEEING INVISIBLE THINGS

As an author and a Christian, I found this collection of fun, rhyming kids' poems an absolute delight. The poems are clever and engaging, the messages are powerful and inspiring, and the illustrations are simply stunning. I highly recommend this book for parents, teachers, and anyone who loves poetry and wants to instill a sense of wonder and faith in young readers.

—**Nick Pirog,** author of *The Speed of Souls*

Lisa's poems for children are full of wonder, beautiful principles, and creativity! Being a mom of two toddlers, I can see how much they learn every day. These readings and poems will serve as an incredible tool for daily reads that provoke the mind and heart!

—**Lindy Cofer,** singer-songwriter @lindy_cofer

As an elementary educator for over ten years, I love how approachable each one of these poems is. They are able to teach big concepts and ideas while maintaining a light sense of fun, which kids of all ages will truly enjoy. I cannot wait to share these poems with my own children!

—**James,** K–5 educator

SEEING INVISIBLE THINGS

SEEING INVISIBLE THINGS

Poems for All of God's Children

WRITTEN & ILLUSTRATED BY

LISA AMBLER

REDEMPTION PRESS

© 2024 Grace Creations. All rights reserved.

Published by Redemption Press, PO Box 427, Enumclaw, WA 98022.
360-226-3488

Redemption Press is honored to present this title in partnership with the author. The views expressed or implied in this work are those of the author. Redemption Press provides our imprint seal representing design excellence, creative content, and high-quality production.

Noncommercial interests may reproduce portions of this book without the express written permission of the author, provided the text does not exceed five hundred words. When reproducing text from this book, include the following credit line: "*Seeing Invisible Things* by Lisa Ambler. Used by permission."

Commercial interests: No part of this publication may be reproduced in any form, stored in a retrieval system, or transmitted in any form by any means—electronic, photocopy, recording, or otherwise—without prior written permission of the publisher/author, except as provided by United States of America copyright law.

All Scripture quotations in this publication are taken from The Holy Bible, New International Version®, NIV® Copyright © 1973, 1978, 1984, 2011 by Biblica, Inc.® Used by permission. All rights reserved worldwide.

ISBN 13 : 978-1-951350-36-9

Library of Congress Catalog Card Number : 2023913865

For more information contact:
artglee@aol.com
info@artforthenations.org
www.artforthe nations.org
www.lisaambler.com

AUTHOR'S NOTE

After raising, teaching, and loving children my entire life, I have learned they are *smart* and often underestimated. I know they love silliness, rhymes, and crazy imagined fantasies, so I have included much of that in this book.

I also know that growing up in this hectic world can feel like an impossible challenge. Suicide rates continue to soar among young people, as do physical and mental stress-related illnesses. It is more crucial than ever to talk about difficult topics with children and encourage them to walk through all challenges with Jesus beside them. I pray some of these poems inspire those important conversations and lead readers to Bible verses full of hope and joy! (Each inspirational verse is listed by the poem.)

Wishing you many blessings and the heart to see them.

Lisa

For my creative, inquisitive, insightful grandchildren,
Trae, Kaleigh, Tre, Eliana, Samara, Lucas,
Josiah, Preston, and Camille
(and their awesome parents, of course)!
With much gratitude to Micah, Lesley, Sara, and all of my editors at
Redemption Press—thank you for your insight,
kindness, and prayers!

Proceeds from this book help
underprivileged children get art supplies.
www.artforthenations.org

The poems in this book are in RFV (Rhyming Fanciful Verse).
Originating over sixty years ago, RFV, like life itself, is full of surprise,
joy, angst, and uneven rhythms.

QUESTIONING SIGHT

We think we are smart, we with sharp eyes,
We who look up and can see the skies.
We who can say without a doubt,
"It won't rain. There are no clouds out."
Then a drop hits our heads, and we cry with surprise,
"That clear blue sky is filled with lies!"
Our false hope is shattered
And all we thought mattered
Has vanished.

Yet we who are smart,
We who see with our hearts,
Will quietly say,
"Sometimes we're wrong
And that is okay."

I Timothy 4:16

Look harder!

13

DAILY

It seems odd
Not to talk about God,
Yet He's absent from most conversations.
People are talking
In all the world's nations
About every want and need.
They are walking
With purpose or greed
Toward a thing called success
That causes much stress.
Is that something I have to do?
I could make a different choice
And use my strong, youthful voice
To speak of all things new,
Like the hope promised everyone
With the rising of each morning sun
As God's mercies are given to me and you!

Lamentations 3:22–23

TRANSPARENT AIR

Our world is ruled by invisible things,
What we do every moment, what each day brings.
For example, you see, we are governed by air.
Whether hot or cold, or blowing our hair,
We have to be in it, we can't get away.
It surrounds us in sleep, it covers our play.
It tugs a new kite right out of our hand
And spreads flower seeds all over the land.
Air does not love, it never hates
But only creates.
A reminder that God
Breathed life into us.

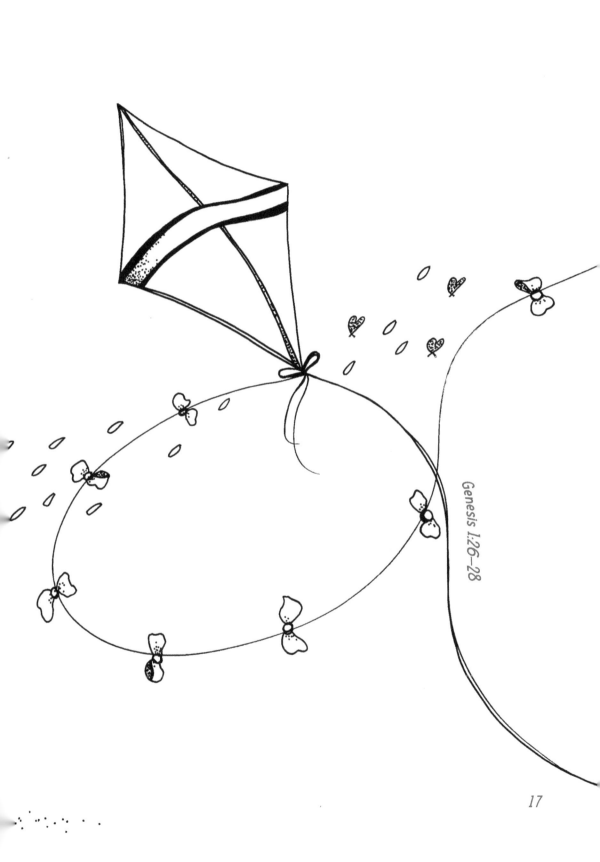

Genesis 1:26–28

REAL WHEEL POWER

Fast and faster, really quick,
If I got to choose, I'd always pick
Traveling on wheels.
When I was an infant, I couldn't walk.
Then it took me a while to speak up and talk
And say what I want.
Now that I can, I am telling you this,
Please listen well, so you don't miss
The brilliance of my thoughts:
"We should be born with wheels on our feet!"
(I do know this sounds a little offbeat.)

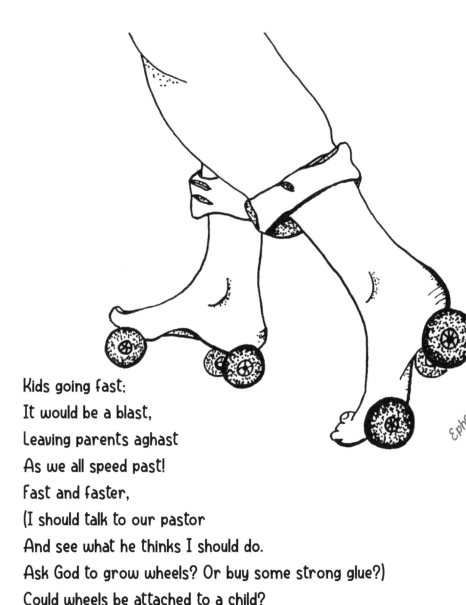

Ephesians 5:15–17

Kids going fast:
It would be a blast,
Leaving parents aghast
As we all speed past!
Fast and faster,
(I should talk to our pastor
And see what he thinks I should do.
Ask God to grow wheels? Or buy some strong glue?)
Could wheels be attached to a child?
Is that a crazy idea, too silly, too wild?
Everyone says to think big and work hard,
To dream giant dreams way beyond your backyard.
Well, let me tell you once again:
Wheels on kids, not "if" but "when"!

HIGGLEDY

"Higgledy piggledy moppin top,"
This is what you say
When your life feels crazy.
There is no other way!
Or "Waggledy paggledy hippin skip"
When you are feeling sad.
"Smuggledy truggle boffle flot"
Seems to work when you're mad.
"Fleepledy neep jeeping bleep"
Chases frowns away.
And "Globbledy wock poomet"
Makes others want to play.
Then,
    When
The awful, terrible grumpies come out,
It's mandatory to stand and shout,
"Higgledy piggledy waggledy paggledy

Smuggledy truggle woo!
Moppin top and hippin skip boffle flot kazoo,
Fleepledy neep and jeeping bleep
Globbledy wock poomet!"
Saying these words together
Might make you break a sweat,
But you'll be feeling better;
That's the point of it all.
So if anyone calls you foolish
Or even an oddball,
Tell them being eccentric
Is the best a person can be,
Because everyone's created
To be their kind of "me"!
God created each one of us
In an extraordinary way,
To be filled with joy about our gifts
And use them every day.

Ephesians 2:10

THERE WILL BE NOODLES

If you are a kid or know of one,
Or were a kid when the world was young,
You've probably encountered noodles
By oodles.
Noodles are what kids like to eat,
With butter or cheese, mmm, what a treat!
Forget about serving fanciful things
Like pickled beets or beans with strings.
Forget about plates and goblets that break.
Kids only need bowls for goodness' sake!
For dessert it is simple. We need cake or ice cream.
Add some cookies to make life a dream.
Kids are not hard, not complicated,
But forgetful adults get mad and frustrated
Because they don't remember their past noodles
By oodles and buttery oodles.

Psalm 107:8—9

SPELLING CLUE

Do you think God has a favorite creature,
One He loves best in every feature?
Ponder the gifts He has given each one;
Some can climb trees, and others can run.
Think of the way each kind was made,
To lie in the sun or to hide in the shade.
Lions majestic with thick, flowing manes.
Earthworms pale, slimy, and plain.
Peacocks dazzling, their blues and greens bright.
Eagles impressive in confident flight.
Which one could God pick as best
Since He made them all, and all by Him are blessed?
Well, if we remember our most-loved pet,
The one every intelligent child wants to get,
The one who is loyal and faithful and true,
Maybe, then, we would have a clue
That, at first, might seem very odd.
But "dog" written backward spells G-O-D, "God"!

Matthew 6:26

Philippians 4:6–7

NOT SO!

I gave half of my sandwich to the new girl in school.

To let her go hungry would have been cruel.

Now my friends are laughing at me,

Saying she and I are kissing in a tree!

"Not so,"

I say, and they should know

I did what was kind and right.

So let's not argue or get in a fight.

I want to be brave—

Not be enslaved

By worldly words—

Since my heart is heard

In heaven.

STOP TALK POP

My brain is busy, I know it is.
Thoughts come out like bubbles, like fizz!
Wild ideas that want to be heard
Burst out before others can utter a word.
And that's not polite,
It isn't right
To be the only one talking.
When I'm with a friend
My opinions don't end.
So I must remember: I should not forget,
That what others say is never a threat
To what I believe.
God gave us our talents, our wonderful gifts,
To use with all people—not to cause rifts.
While great conversations do come from the tongue,
It's best to learn this truth while you are young:
The smartest person uses his ears!
Talk with your mouth, then listen with patience.
Respect everyone, be kind, be gracious.
Talk and then stop
While ideas pop
From everyone's heads.

Proverbs 10:19

MURDER!

Have you ever murdered?
In anger, thought to kill?
"No," you answer quickly,
"I could not and never will!"
I believe you do respect another's life;
I know you wouldn't shoot someone
Or stab them with a knife.
But when your friends get something
That you wish you had,
Do you try to kill their joy by making them feel bad?
Are you ever jealous when someone wins a prize?
Do you stop their praises with your jeering cries?
If only you could realize this important fact
And use it as the rule before making an attack:
A death of any kind cannot be undone.
When the dying happens, nobody has won.
Killing happiness, like the taking of a life,
Ends in fruitless tiredness, all-exhausting strife.
Cheering great achievements and providential blessing
Will fill you with pure joy through the love you are expressing.
Celebrate everyone's triumphs! Cheer when anyone wins!
Bring balloons! Throw confetti! Rejoice and be glad!

1 Peter 2:1

GAIN

While much proves true and worthy
During this time called life,
It also can be hard.
We learn there are blessings
Mixed with pain and strife
And grow tired.
But all success and failure matters not one bit.
All the things we started or were forced to quit
Have meaning through our heart's intent.
All is gained through love.
Truly, love is God.

I Corinthians 13

THE GENESIS OF AIR

In the beginning, the genesis,
God made invisible air.
I can imagine it went like this:
He used songs and laughter, then knit them with care
So that every breath taken
Would become
A joy awakened
In everyone.

Trees in the wind,
Which was air playing rough,
Would bend
Just enough
To show they shared
A life influenced
By air.
To all not convinced
Of miraculous things,
God taught every bird
To fly airborne with wings.
Have you not heard?
Our God is mercy; our God is grace.
He gave His very breath
For the earth's whole space
To inhale until bodily death.
Then do not despair
Beyond our time here, through all afterward,
Our spirits will live in God's heavenly air
And, laughing, exhale His bright words.

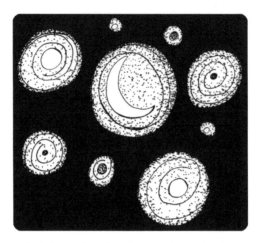

THE GENESIS OF STARS

In the beginning, the genesis,
God made millions of brilliant stars twinkling.
I can imagine it went like this:
Reaching into night skies,
He gave them a sprinkling
Of light shaped round by His hands.
So darkness complete
Would not cover the lands.
So dreams would be sweet
During each person's sleep
As they passed the night
Knowing God's love would keep
Shining pure light
Through all of their life.
And each earthly hour,
Each blessing, each strife,
Would be touched by His power.

Genesis 1:5

THE GENESIS OF WATER

In the beginning, the genesis,
God made water, sparkling, pure.
I can imagine it went like this:
He found all things blue, I am sure,
Then mixed in sprinkles
Of white and green
So there would be twinkles
In each watery scene.
He gave life and movement
To the great depth,
A beauty translucent,
Leading to the next step
Where He placed water up in clouds.
Rain kisses the field,
Encouraging crowds
Of plants with their yield
So man could harvest and eat.
Then people could rest,
Dive into a lake's cool retreat.
How God made this wonder, one of His best,
Nobody knows.
I am just blessed
By the bounty sweet water bestows.

Genesis 1:9

THE GENESIS OF OUR WORLD

In the beginning, the genesis,
God made a planet called Earth.
I can imagine it went like this:
He gathered together things of great worth,
Like rocks and trees,
With a blue sky above,
Making beauty to please——
A location to love.
He sculpted giant peaks.
He planted the field,
Then set water in creeks
To nurture the yield.
He wrapped it 'round in air so pure
It could spin in space,
Steady and sure.
With benevolent grace,
God said it was good
And that He would rest
Then shepherd, He would
This planet most blessed.

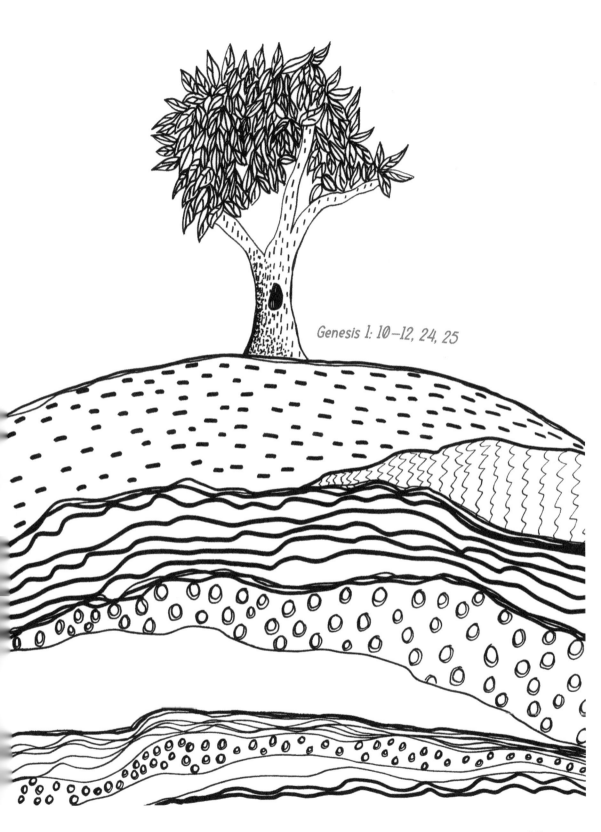

Genesis 1: 10–12, 24, 25

THE GENESIS OF CREATURES

In the beginning, the genesis,
God made all kinds of creatures.
I can imagine it went like this:
He had great fun inventing their features
And giving them talents to thrive.
He created each one unique,
With a voice to show they're alive.
Tiny ones making a squeak,
Larger animals roaring,
Some flapping feathered wings
And into the blue sky soaring.
Some given sharpened teeth,
Others a vicious sting,
So each has the tools for survival
In this imperfect place
That solemnly awaits the arrival
Of our Savior's healing grace.
Yet surely all creatures are knowing
The touch of their Creator's hand
With every step of paws and claws showing
Heavenly instincts leading
Through the dry, hardened land.

Genesis 1:25

THE GENESIS OF PEOPLE

In the beginning, the genesis,
God made Adam, then Eve.
I can imagine it went like this:
Knowing what He would achieve,
God took dust from the ground
And formed a man,
Filled lungs with air, a holy sound,
And that is how our life began.
Created to work in teams,
To live free
With our hopes and our dreams.
To be
In step with our Maker, our Lord.
Walking with Him,
Not alone or ignored.
Designed, not made on a whim.
To search
For joy, fulfillment, and peace,
Within this world, our church,
Until our earthly days cease.
Then our spirit that came from God's breath,
Will lead us home,
After corporeal death,
To know fully, be loved, and be known.

Genesis 1:26–30

WHEN I PRAY

I prayed my sick mom could get out of bed,
That dad would lovingly kiss her head,
That my family would have enough money to pay
For more than just the needs of one day.
When I pray, I know my God hears,
But when things don't get better, I fear
I did not pray
Just the right way
Or often enough.
Then Mom smiles bravely and says to me;
"Remember, for this world God made us to be
Free, not perfect
But perfectly free,
Knowing all will be well eternally.
When everything's wrong and nothing feels right,
Ask to see a glimpse of His light,
Because God's pure love shines brighter than hate,
Brighter than problems small and great,
And just bright enough so we can view
Our promised future, joyous and new.
So look with your heart and know in your soul
That all of God's children will soon be whole.
Your prayers are answered."

James 5:13

41

WAIT!

Of all the things children hate
(And most people too),
Being told to sit and wait
Is "number one don't want to do!"
Yet as we go about our busy day,
Often forgetting to stop and pray,
God waits patiently for us.
God is love, and love is always patient.

1 Corinthians 13

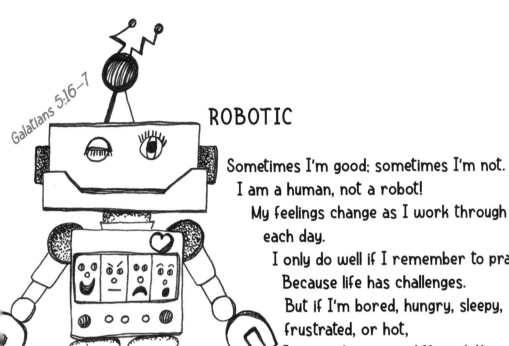

Galatians 5:16–7

ROBOTIC

Sometimes I'm good; sometimes I'm not.
I am a human, not a robot!
My feelings change as I work through
each day.
I only do well if I remember to pray.
Because life has challenges.
But if I'm bored, hungry, sleepy,
frustrated, or hot,
I may act in ways different than
taught.
Then I must pause and take a time-out,
Say I am sorry, smile and not pout.
But that's all right.
Having emotions is no shame.
It's how we react and then accept blame
For mistakes we have made.
Even Jesus got angry and tired,
Yet He did all His Father required.
And he was humble.
Having no moods would be robotic,
Unrealistic, and a bit idiotic!
I just need to ask God for help each day
To do my best.
Amen! OK!

LIFE TIME

Well, it's high time to talk about this,
To make a rhyme you cannot dismiss.
Grandpas and moms, young children and teens,
All talk about what passing time means.
Some kids are impatient to grow up and be
Able to do what they please and be free.
Teens want to drive their very own car.
Parents dream of a break to travel afar.
It seems everyone hurries and all forget
To enjoy this moment before the sunset.
Your job now, as a wise young person,
Is to help the world out before things worsen!
Teach all those you know how to watch ants
As they carry a leaf across your pants.
Teach them to look for shapes in the clouds,
To stop and slow down, get out of the crowds.
To gently pull petals off a full pink rose,
Then flutter them down so they tickle your nose.
Tell them nothing true changes, but everything will
If they don't learn to listen, be quiet, and hold still,
While God lets the world spin in His hands
And sunbeams travel across many lands.

Because He gave this world to us just for a minute,
The short, quick time we will be in it
Is a gift to be savored
In all of its flavors.

James 4:13–14

BEYOND BEGINNING

It's a simple question to ask,
Answering a difficult task,
Who made God?
God is the constant who made what came after.
He created this world and us, filled with laughter.
God is the Maker.
"Always" means a thing that did not begin—
It is and was and continuously has been.
God is always.
"Forever" is something that will never end—
Upon that fact we can depend.
God is forever.
But how do we know He's been eternally there,
Existing before anything, even the air?
We know because we are alive.
We are real people, humans, it's true:
If we were nothing, there's nothing we could do!
"Nothing" is zero.
And zero times zero will always be
The absence of anything created and free
To be thankful.

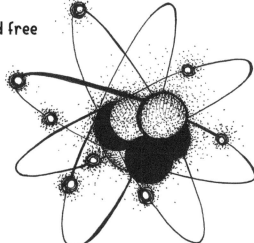

Revelation 22:13

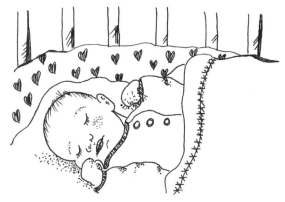

Matthew 18:10
Psalm 4:8

HELPLESS

It is weird to know, as I read this verse,
I was once small enough to fit in a purse!
Baby-me could not walk
Or comprehensibly talk
To tell anyone I was thinking,
"My diaper is wet and stinking!"
When I was hungry, I could not say,
"Hey, get me a pizza if that's okay."
I could not stand up. If you sat me down,
I flopped on my side and wailed with a frown.
When I was so tiny my head couldn't lift,
I think my survival was truly a gift
From our loving God.
And it wouldn't be odd
For angels to have been in my room,
Keeping me safe so I could bloom
And thrive, be alive,
To be thankful.
I lie down and sleep peacefully, for you, Lord, make me safe.

JAGGED

My brother and his best friend like to stand outside
Hurling rocks across the street to hit a pole that's wide.
They say it builds their muscles and sharpens up their aim,
And when there's not much else to do, it's an interesting game.
Once, while I was watching them, a sharp rock struck that pole.
And bouncing back to hit my head——it made a bloody hole.
Our mom came running to us when she heard me crying.
Then, gently wiping off the blood, she said this, all while sighing,
"Don't you children know that when you're throwing things,
There is a danger they'll take off, as if on tiny wings,
Causing pain and damage wherever they may strike
And doing harm to others in ways you wouldn't like?"
My brother shouted back, "My stupid friend, not me,
Threw that rock so hard. I'm not to blame, you see."
There was silence for a moment before my mother talked,
As with her hands on both of the boys,
Across the street they walked.

"Now you've each thrown hurt; you've caused each other pain.
Using ugly words leaves nothing to gain.
Jesus tells all people to be very sure
To throw things at others only if you're pure.
And none of us is perfect; none is always right.
So we should never toss things. Do you see the light?"
"Yes, ma'am," the boys said,
"And we're sorry about her head!"
Whew! Good thing!
(But time out anyway.)

John 8:7

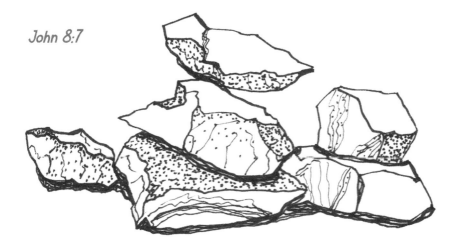

OTHER'S EYES

I stood ready to run
Quickly across the street.
I couldn't wait for anyone
Because I needed to eat!
Then I noticed an older man,
Wobbling where he stood.
He held a cane in one hand
And said, "I don't feel good."
I took a breath and then replied,
"I will help you if I can."
"Oh thank you," he then cried.
So we walked hand in hand.
With slow, deliberate care.
"Just when I think I can't,"
He said, "possibly go anywhere,
A stranger like you is kind
To me, a person who is blind."
I looked at him with my bright eyes
And said, "Sir, don't worry.
Really, I have time; there is no
      huge hurry."
Being kind is love.
      God is lovingly kind.

1 Corinthians 13

LOLLIPOP REVIVAL

I'd like to lick a lollipop
Every single day
'Cause when I lick a lollipop,
My troubles go away!
Likely, licking lollipops
Boosts the power of your brain,
'Cause when you lick a lollipop
Crazy things seem sane.
My cousin's not allowed to lick.
His mom says it is germy,
That licking things will make him sick
Or even make him wormy!
Ick!
But if the whole world licked a lollipop
Every single day,
If everyone could only stop
And take the time to pray,
Life would be sweet!
Neat!

John 14:27

LION TAMER

I can't help it. I am wild
When I am NOT the birthday child!
Watching a gift be unwrapped by my aunt,
My face frowns. I start to pant.
Eating cake made for my brother,
I choke and think I would rather
Eat dirt!
I can't help it; I feel sick
When happy people have a lick
Of someone else's birthday ice cream!
I just want to scream.
It's not my fault. It's beyond my control
When jealous feelings swallow me whole
Like a boa constrictor!
But just like a mouse
And a snake in your house
Can't make their home in the same cage,
Neither can kindness dwell with rage.
If I grab those feelings so wild in my heart,
Put them away, just for a start,
And be kind,
Soon the praise I will get for being so sweet
Will fill me with joy much better than treats.
And the wild raging beast will be tamed.

Proverbs 14:30

BOASTFUL

"I'm taller than you,"
She said with glee,
"And I look good in blue!"
"Oh, who cares?" asked he.
"That's silly to brag about
Or even have any pride.
You can't control when you sprout,
Even if you tried!"
So when you're tempted to crow
About being big or smart or great,
God says to be slow,
To be humble and wait,
To compliment someone else.
Love does not envy or boast;
Love is not proud, and it does not dishonor others.
God is perfect love,
And He loves us perfectly!

I Corinthians 13

OH MISTER, IF YOU KNEW MY SISTER

While sitting in the office at my elementary school,
I feel sorry, just a little bit, for acting such a fool.
I did throw the eraser that hit the teacher's face,
But I wasn't aiming at her. My pitch was a disgrace!
I could not bear to listen while she sang my sister's praises
And named her "student of the year" with enthusiastic phrases.
Because, you see, my sister is really not a saint—
If I told you what she did at home, it would make you faint.
At home she snatches my best toys and hides them all away,
Then tells me I can have them back if I play with her all day.
And if I play "her way"!
Now the principal is calling me, so I tell him the whole story.
How my sister acts so perfect, winning all the glory.
He thinks for a long while, and then he says to me,
"You did throw that eraser and owe an apology.
I'd like for you to see me after school is out.
I'm sure that you can be of use; of that, I have no doubt."
During the next week, I help the office staff.
I learn to file and copy things, even take a photograph!
On my last day of work, the staff hands me a sign:
"Super-Office-Helper with Gifts that Truly Shine."
The principal clears his throat, and then he says to me,
"You did well this week; now I have to make a plea:

John 8:7

56

Please remember that each person has their natural skills,
God-given talents to use as they will.
So when you feel jealous of what others get,
Think of what you have right now and what you can do yet.
With patience and with time,
Tall heights you will climb!"
I think I understand now what life is all about.
It's being glad of who you are and working through all doubt.
Because if everyone was a teacher, and there were no good cooks,
Then we would have to eat the paper pages from our study books!
If all people worked in offices, and no one planted flowers,
Then there would be no pretty parks to play in for long hours.
My sister is quite special but not the same as me.
She can sit and read while I want to climb a tree.
So as we get older and learn more things to do,
We will go far together as a team of two.
God made people different so they each could learn
Their need for others and then to yearn
For Him.

Psalm 139:14

THE HARD WAY

If there were no people who dared to do good,
I would have died long before I should
For not listening.
The water was glistening in the pool,
Blue and shining like a jewel.
So my toddler-self jumped in
And, not knowing how to swim, I sank.
A man jumped in, giving my arm a yank,
And hurled me back on dry ground
Just as my mom turned around.
"I said, 'Stay put for just one minute
While I blow up this raft to put you in it,'"
She shouted.
I pouted
Because we went home.
Then I sat alone
In my room to cough
While I dried off
And thought about learning to listen.

Proverbs 1:5

58

ANOTHER PAINFUL LESSON

Kids have to go to school
Or else grow up like fools!
But sometimes, learning is hard.
You spend hours adding, reading, and writing,
Then run to the playground, where some kids start fighting.
Stressful!
Once at recess, a girl pulled my hair
Right out of my scalp, leaving it bare
Above one eye.
It made me cry. Then I punched her hard and made her fall.
My right hand smashed into the brick wall
And broke with a crack.
I should not have struck back.
It was a painful, awful lesson.
In my heart I heard God speak.
"You should have turned the other cheek."
Well, amen to that!

Matthew 5:39

GERMS

Cover your face! Sneeze in your shirt!
Wash your hands! Don't play in the dirt!
So many people in so many ways
Fret about germs through all of their days.
Now, I do know they're real
And can make you feel
Quite sick, quite quick.
It's good to stay clean and eat healthy stuff
And exercise lots so you will be tough.
Then germs may bounce right off your skin,
Or if they get in,
You will heal fast
And the sickness won't last.
And, dear one, most important of all,
God cares about you and won't let you fall
Without helping as you struggle,
Holding you close like a warm snuggle.
He knows how many hairs grow on your head,
How tall you are, what fills you with dread.
Worry instead about every germ?
I would rather eat a fat worm!
Raw!

Psalm 94:19

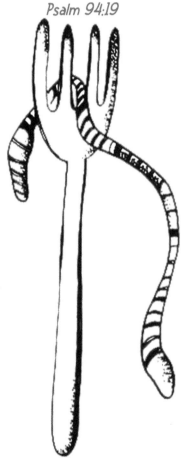

INCONVENIENT

I want you to know it's a pain in my classes
To always be keeping up with my glasses!
When the weather is hot, they slip down my nose.
I look down, they fall off and land at my toes
Because I am wet with sweat!
When winter comes, and ice covers the ground,
They fly from a snowball, not to be found
Until spring, when little birds sing.
Whatever the season
And reason
Or not,
I often can't see well because I forgot
To bring them from where they lay in the night,
Glinting at me if I can't get it right,
And remember to take them and clean them with care,
Then remember to bring them everywhere.
But I am lucky to have them at all,
To see this world's wonders, the big and the small,
To see the smile on my mother's face

Luke 18:43

When we gather for dinner and say our day's
grace.
I am blessed to have vision;
God's provision
For me is that I open my eyes,
And I can see.

61

FANTASTICAL BEASTS

Since the very day I was born,
I have wanted a unicorn.
Either I'm told there are none
Or that they are too wild
And the horn too sharp for me, a child.
My brother says he would trade his red wagon
To meet a friendly fire-breathing dragon.
Either he's told there are none
Or that such dangerous flames
Would not be allowed in children's games.
Adults may say these creatures aren't real
Or that the rules they defy have rebel appeal,
And lead us to believe in impossible things,
Like sugar-spun castles with benevolent kings.
They distract us from learning an important truth:
That life is hard after brief youth.
I say instead
These fantastical beasts give more than they take.
To dismiss their value is a mistake.

They teach all children to search for a prize
Between blades of grass, beyond rainbow skies,
For a sparkle of hope, a glimmer of light:
Like Christ, who can turn a wrong into right.
When you believe through all of your days
That God is there each moment, always,
You will get to heaven and might hear Him say,
"Want to ride a unicorn today?"

Matthew 19:26

SACRIFICE

It's one of those words that doesn't sound nice—
"Sacrifice."
So I looked it up in the dictionary.
It sounds scary!
Giving a dead animal to God?
That cannot be right; it sounds too odd.
My dad said that was before Christ came
And died for us; now we pray in His name.
Jesus died, then rose alive,
So one day we could arrive
At the gates of heaven unstained,
By the blood of death unchained
From the bonds of sin.
We will joyfully enter in!
But why was this all necessary?
Is God being mean or contrary?
Is He just acting like a king
Who's in control of everything?
No way, I say,
And know in my heart.
This plan gives us a start
Toward understanding Him.
It wasn't a silly whim

But a plan for happiness.
If we learn to be content and grateful,
Love each other and not be hateful,
We will see a glimmer of God's pure light.
That is why this plan is right:
By giving
We are living
The best kind of life.

Romans 10:9; Psalm 51

HUNTING

It's almost time to hunt Easter eggs,
So I've started building strength in my legs.
I want to take the most.
I don't even want to be close
To second place.
Last year my youngest cousin won.
I remember it clearly.
It was not fun.
This year I'll knock those little kids over
And let them fall with a splat into the
   clover.
While I grab them all—the purple, the pink,
The blue, the yellow—I'll make a stink
If anyone else gets more.
I want to be the winner!
Does that make me a sinner?
Love is not self-seeking; it is not easily
   angered;
It keeps no record of wrongs.
God's love shares everything, even Easter candy.

1 Corinthians 13

ARMED

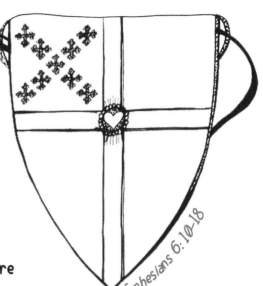

Ephesians 6:10-18

Different kids through different
    stages,
Carry different things through different
    ages.
But all are armed.
He carried his teddy. She carried her doll.
They took them everywhere when they were
    small
And felt safe.
Then she strapped a purse over her shoulder.
He carried a backpack when they were older
And felt hopeful.
Then they carried computers and intelligent phones,
Gym clothes and books, heavy like stones,
And felt overwhelmed.
They got bigger but not big enough
To handle this world and all of its stuff,
Until they emptied their hands.
Hands that were empty could clasp in prayer
Or grasp a friend to support them and share
The danger of life.
They prayed for God's armor to shield them with truth,
For His wisdom to guide them through perils of youth,
And now they stand strong.

Hebrews 10:35-36

BETWEEN RAINDROPS

If you try to do tasks that are really quite hard,
Like building a treehouse in your backyard,
People might laugh.
Then they will ask, looking askew,
"What exactly, little one, are you trying to do?"
"Kids are too young to hammer sharp, pointed nails,"
They will explain, while your face pales.
"Too small."
"Too weak."
"Too uneducated."
They may say things that make you feel hated.
So gather your wits and stand up straight.
Look in their eyes and say this; don't wait:
"I am tiny enough to do HUGE things
One step at a time because I have wings
To soar through the world up to the bright sky,
Small enough to dance between raindrops when I try."

GAME TIME

I need to play
For hours each day!
On the screen,
I mean,
Where I can kill
Just for the thrill,
Where I can drive at high speed,
Collect money with greed,
Pass every test—

Be the best of the best!
Or stop and reset,
Then quickly forget
That I lost,
Because here there's no cost.
Except maybe my brain
Could start to retrain
In a way that's not actually true.
Real tasks to get through

Might be too much

If I don't have the crutch

Of one click to erase my mistakes.

I might not have what it takes

To live and be brave,

To behave

Like Christ Jesus our Lord,

Hated instead of adored.

He gave Himself without fear

And rose from the dead to always be near

So our time will end

In an eternal win.

If I remember that life is no game,

To fight every battle by calling His name,

And use my free will

To love and not kill,

Then I am a hero.

My score never zero

But soaring way over the top

With a God who can never be stopped!

Proverbs 24:16; James 1:22–24

ISAIAH'S WORDS

Grownups say kids are too energetic.

Adults can't keep up; it's just pathetic.

But kids get exhausted too. Life is hard, with so much to do.

Kids are always expected to grow.

To improve our skills and the things that we know.

To run and not trip, to walk and not fall,

To eat well, stand straight, so we'll grow tall.

It's a lot to do on our own. Can we do it alone?

Have you not heard Isaiah's words?

They were written a long time ago,

When people were feeling quite tired and low.

God never grows weary, Isaiah said.

God never sleeps—He does not go to bed!

Young people should know they can stumble,

Mess up, make mistakes, and take a big tumble

God will be there forgiving,

To give you reasons for living

And trying.

He helps you stop crying.

72

He gives strength to the weary
And love to the teary.
Soon you'll feel ready to soar,
To fly through trials and open each door!
Isaiah's promise is real,
No matter how you may feel.
For thousands of years,
Through troubles and fears,
Millions of girls and boys
Have relied on these words to block out the noise
Of discouragement, failure, and dread.
So read them tonight as you go to bed.
And be blessed.

Isaiah 40:28–31

SCREEN TIME

Let me have more screen time.
Then my life will be fine.
Let me stay hooked to the internet.
I know to be careful: it won't be a threat.
Let my friends and the whole world see
That I am cool and smart and free!
I will show off my hair, colored green and blue,
The ring in my nose and a neck tattoo.
No worries, for sure, these things won't be real.
I can change them all daily just by how I feel.
The computer is magic; it can add and delete
Until the photo of me is movie-star sweet.
Of course, when I've tweaked each bit of me,
Made things so perfect they could never be,
I'll have to stay in my room
Until it feels like a tomb
For the lonesome, flawed,
Needing God
To feel loved,
Really, really real-me.

Joshua 1:9

74

NOT LIKELY

The villain in a movie laughs his evil laugh
As he thinks about cutting the hero in half.
Horrible!
He hisses, "I'll get rid of him for good,
As a guy like me should,
And then I can rule the world! Hah!"
"That's not likely," the hero replies.
"Good always wins every prize
In the end,
My wicked friend."
Only love is eternal, and that's the truth.
God is love.

POOR KID

People think of money whenever they hear "poor,"
But as Jesus knows, it can mean something more.
Often the richest monied people, those who brag and boast,
Are the people who feel worthless, the ones who hurt the most.
To feel like you have nothing to offer to this earth
Is worse than being hungry because you doubt your worth.
To feel like you have nobody in your life to care
Is worse than losing all your clothes, everything you wear.
And when you are mourning, feeling truly sad,
When your heart is hurting, only Jesus makes you glad.
Because being truly wealthy
Is having a spirit that is healthy.
Millions can be wasted on expensive, fragile stuff.
If you keep on buying things, you'll never get enough.
You could brag about your street style and your four-carat ring,
Telling everyone who listens that soon you will be king.
But instead of spending money when you're feeling down,
Pray for heaven's riches to turn your day around.
You're more valuable than diamonds when you walk with Christ,
More important than anything, "#high-priced"!
No bragging necessary!
The humble are blessed indeed
Because our mighty God fulfills every need!

Matthew 5:3–4

EEEEK!

What does it mean to be meek?
And why should I be that way?
I think it means timid and weak,
Not a trait that would help with my day!
All I hear is to be proud
In everything I do,
Stand for my rights and shout loud;
Tell everyone my views.
But Jesus stayed humble and gentle,
Even as He faced death,
Keeping a strength that was mental
As He took his final breath.
He could have called all of the angels
To strike His accusers down.
Instead He hung broken and mangled,
Mocked by all around.
That's what it means to be meek and kind
When others are not,
Using strength within your mind, acting as you've been taught.

Weak people can't do what they should,

Or they just don't try;

Choosing evil instead of good

Because it's an easier lie.

If you are wronged in this life, but you choose to endure

With patience, mercy, and grace,

God will know your heart is pure.

He will say that you won the race;

Your life was a job well done,

As you sit with Him in a heavenly place,

Your joyful riches won!

Matthew 5:5

Matthew 5:5

EMPTY

I hear a rumbling down in my tummy,
That means I need food, warm and yummy:
Macaroni and cheese,
If you please!
Sometimes I eat plenty but feel hollow and bare,
Unfilled and naked despite the clothing I wear.
I feel like there's a hole in my body,
Where goodness leaks out after I've been naughty.
I feel worthless and angry, sad and afraid;
I can't be my best self until I have prayed,
"Lord, fill me up with mercy and love.
Give me forgiveness that comes from above."
Then I will not be empty.

UNSQUISHED

Sometimes when I see a snail and its slimy trail,
I feel like squishing it flat.
Until I start to think about that,
The violence I would be committing.
Then I look at the snail while I am sitting.
Four pale tentacles wave at me—
Two that can smell and two that can see.
I study the shell and notice how well
It sits on the snail's slippery back.
I cannot attack
This tiny life form,
Not while my heart is beating and warm.
Sometimes when I see a kid fumble a ball,
Or trip when they're walking down the school hall,
I want to laugh out loud,
Because I am feeling so proud
That they messed up, not me.
Until I remember to be
Helpful and kind
Since soon I may find,
The person making mistakes,
Whose heart truly aches,
Who needs compassion,
Is me.
To be unsquished—that's mercy!

Matthew 5:6

OLIVE BRANCH

Up four steps sits my brother;
Five steps beyond, I am still.
We are obeying our mother—
Of our fighting, she's had her fill!
Whenever we clash and battle
Over toys or games we're playing,
She silently points, not letting us tattle,
To the stairs where we will be staying.
She hands us each a green paper square
To hold and to fold while we sit,
Reminding us not to go anywhere
Until we calm down a bit.
We take this paper scrap
And crease it to look like a leaf,
So it will become a treasure map
And lead to the end of our grief.
Like the new-sprouted branch after the flood,
This sliver of green symbolizes
The forgiveness that came after Christ shed His blood,
The most valuable of all prizes.
So when we are calm and can speak
An apology heartfelt and true,

When we can each offer our cheek
To be kissed, then we can start anew.
And a peace passing all understanding
Will fill us with happiness,
No longer will we be demanding
Our way, because we are blessed.

Matthew 5.9

LAUNDERED

I love a white T-shirt
When it's brand new,
Without stains or dirt.
But whatever I do,
I cannot keep it clean!
Do you know what I mean?
I love a new day
When I'm just starting out
To work or to play
With no reason to pout
Or shout a mean word
That is heard
To the heavens.
Ugliness seems to slip from my lips.
But when I look in my heart, I feel sure
That because of Christ's love, I am pure.
Wash me clean inside out, Lord, and then,
I can start my time over again
And shine!

Matthew 5:8

FRAIL FRIENDS

There is a girl who lives on our street.
She's the sister of two of my friends.
She is cheerful and kind, funny and sweet,
But after those things, our likeness ends.
She cannot walk; her hands don't work well.
She can't skip rope.
She can't run; she can't yell.
Yet she holds on to hope
That every day, we will include her in all games we play.
Other kids living nearby
Make fun of me
When I try
To be
    Patient and loving and stay behind,
       When others don't care
          That she's confined
            To a wheelchair.
            They call me "sissy," "silly," and "weak."
           I try not to listen, try not to speak.
           Instead I remember the clear words of Christ
            Saying we will be honored for all sacrificed
             In doing what's right.

Matthew 5:10–12

HAIR

If you look at it one way, boys are lucky:
They can cut their hair short before it gets yucky!
I guess girls can do that as well,
But most of us seem to love hair spray and gel.
As they say in that famous song,
Most of us like it long
And shining, streaming, gleaming,
Growing down to there.
Hair!
Easier said than done.
Doing my hair is often not fun.
It must be braided tight to my head
And put in a cap when I go to bed
Lest it get frizzy,
Making me dizzy
And shout when tangles come out!
The hair of a Black girl is hard to get right.
Doing it well can take the whole night!
My best friend laughs when I gripe about hair.
She says I know nothing and should be aware
That my hair is thick, not thin and sad.
She thinks her straight hair is always bad.
Because Asian hair is straight and slick—

Luke 12:7

Combing it out, easy and quick.

But it's always the same,

Neat, shiny, and tame!

My other friend's hair is red, really bright,

With curls too, some loose, some tight.

She says it has an Irish mind,

So she's become resigned

To leaving it alone

To do what it wants on its own!

Hey! Maybe that's the best plan:

To let our hair do what it can

And not fight

For what we think is right

Or stylish because

When it is cut, it's all just fuzz!

TANGLED ROOTS

My family tree has tangled roots,
Standing tall and lopsided with unknown fruits.
It is not very pretty but sturdy, well made,
To give those standing under protection
    and shade.
Some in my family were not very nice.
Some even were criminals and paid the price.
Some who are living are loving and fun;
Others aren't happy with all they have
    done.
Some call me "sweetie," giving
    kisses and hugs;
Others straighten my clothes with
    angry tugs.
My mom and my dad are no longer married.
Their schedules are hectic; they feel tired and
    harried.
At family parties, some people fight.
Others get silly and drink beer all night.
So I often feel sad.
Is my family bad?
Then I remember ancestors we share,
The hard things they fought through, the
    love and despair.

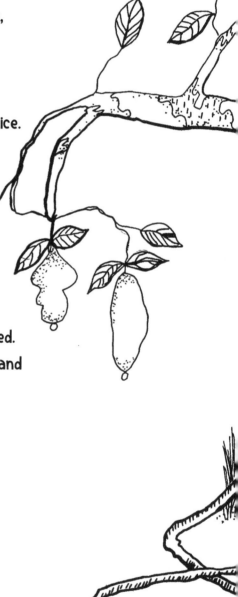

Adam and Eve, Noah, Mary, and John—
  Their stories remind me that though they are gone,
    Their family tree is also mine.
            And each night, as the stars shine,

I remember God's promise to Abraham
And that I am a true child of God, yes, I am!

Genesis 22:17

SOUNDINGS

Listen, if you have ears that hear,
To sounds around you, both far and
near.
Close your eyes just for a bit
    While you rest. Take a moment to sit.
        There are natural noises like those
            from the wind,
                Making leaves chitter as dry
                branches bend.
Waters from rivers and fat raindrops
Splash and crash in tinkles and plops.
The gruff rumble and grumble of
    neighboring dogs
Drowns out the chirruping croak
    of frogs.
In the busy life of God's creation,
Listen!
There are manmade clamors from saws,
    from hammers.

Trucks and cars screech, then beep.
A baby wails, awakened from sleep.
A lady outside is sweeping and singing
While the tintinnabulation of church bells ringing
Fills the air of God's creation.
Listen!
What kind of noises do you make each day?
Do you speak gentle words at work and at play?
Do you pause before speaking and think what words mean?
To those who will hear them, are they sweet or obscene?
If you were to measure the depth of your chatter,
Would you be saying things that matter?
If you were to probe then explore every word,
Would your conversation be wise or absurd?
Try to listen within the quiet of your heart.
Think of your sounds before they start.
Then know your voice is music to God.
He listens.

James 1:19

STRESSFUL QUESTIONS

Why in the world would someone ask,
"What will you do when you're grown?"
Just growing up is a challenging task:
I have to do all on my own.
Today I think a firefighter
Because I am feeling brave.
I could hold the hose tighter
While others watch and wave.
I could be a priest, a librarian,
Or if you are keeping score,
I could even be a contrarian,
Fighting for good on the Senate floor!
Tomorrow I might be tired, unsure of what I could do,
Thinking too much is required to be an adult like you.
Ask me easy questions, like what I want to eat.
Then I can keep believing
I won't ever face defeat.
And I will be receiving
A valuable gift from you.
I will be given the confidence
To try to conquer things new.
Or tell me about true things,

Since it might take a while to decide
To stand firm on my feet and find wings,
To find the courage inside.
And if you really do care,
As I walk with God through this life,
Always keep me in prayer.
Remind me He will be there
Through easy times and strife.

Psalm 32:8; Job 12:7-10

DANGEROUS WORDS

Here's another idea, the very best yet.
What if we each had a smart talking pet?
We could look into the eyes of our dog, hog, or cat,
Talk about this, chat about that.
And, whenever you had a day that was bad,
Or you felt angry, or worried, and sad,
They would wiggle a bit or cock their cute head
And, listening well to each word you said,
Reply, "Oh, my!"
They might say, "I am sorry that happened to you.
Let's grab cookies: it's a great thing to do."
Even though Mom said, "Too late for treats,"
You and your pet deserve many sweets.
And cookies do make you feel better.
You could hide them under your sweater!
So you swipe several cookies and gobble them down.
Then see your mom as she asks with a frown,
"Are you eating?"
"Hello and yes," your pet says in greeting.
Animals are honest and cannot lie.
Tell an untruth? They would rather die.
It's something to ponder before you get rattled
And mad at your pet because they have tattled.
If they could talk, we would want them to say
That we're worth their love in every way!

Job 12:7–10

REPEATING PETE

I live next door to a beautiful bird
Who only squawks terrible words.
"Bad bird," he says again and once more.
"Bad Bird! Screeeeech!" It's almost a roar.
He is turquoise and yellow,
A quite stunning fellow,
Yet he doesn't know how handsome he looks:
How his praises are written in library books.
This bird named Pete says he is bad
Because that's what he hears from the man who's his dad.
Parrot Pete repeats.
I live down the street
      From a boy also named Pete,
        And, very sadly, he is not sweet!
          He says terrible words to everyone,
          Hits smaller kids, makes the girls run.
          This boy is handsome, but the clothes he wears
           Are tattered and dirty, like nobody cares.

"You're stupid, I hate you,"
He shouts at us all.
He kicks rocks at our feet, making us fall.
I wonder if his mom or his dad
Often tell Pete that he is bad.
Could it be possible he feels hated?
That being unloved makes him frustrated?
Jesus Christ says that when someone is mean,
We should be calm and not cause a scene.
If an unkind person slaps at our face,
We should turn our heads, showing them grace.
I'm not sure I could do that, but for Jesus, I'll try.
Maybe I could walk away as I cry.
Then I will say to myself as I go,
"The poor kid is cruel because that's all he knows."
Pete must have learned to repeat.
And when I say my prayers each night,
I will ask God to make it
All right for Pete.

Ephesians 4:29; Proverbs 18:21

IMMEASURABLE

There are so many miracles in our world,
Way too many to name.
One of the biggest, I think,
Is that no snowflakes are the same.
Tiny, intricate crystals of beauty
Beyond human imagination
Point directly to my Lord,
The origin of all creation.

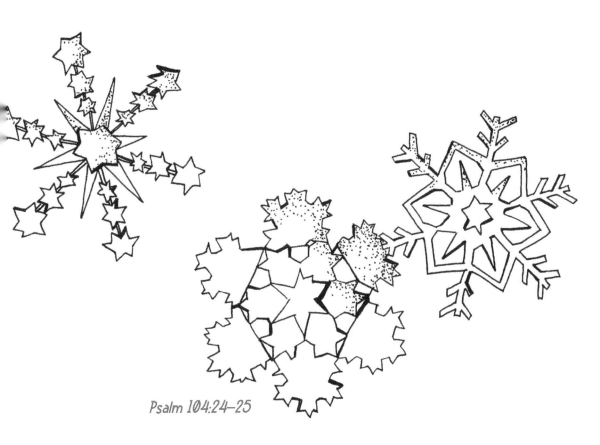

Psalm 104:24–25

NEW KID

The first day at a new school
In a different town
Tends to be very uncool.
It makes me feel down.
I worry a lot
About making new friends.
Will they like me or not?
The angst never ends.
So, I slump down and walk in a stoop
Until I hear laughter, loud and high
From this happy group
And I think I can try.
Then, once again, I stall,
Remembering I'm a mess:
Too skinny, too pale, not very tall
(Again, I feel stress)!
Then one kid peeks out the door.
A girl in a wheelchair,
Then even more,
A tiny brown boy,
Smiles at me, and I dare
To feel joy.
As different kids appear,
Some black, some white, some plump, some thin,
I want to cheer!
I will fit right in!

MATH CLASS

I stare at the numbers I'm supposed to add,
Trying to think,
Not to get mad.
But I'm on the brink of crying.
Three numbers sit in a row,
Four more digits below,
Then five numbers with a minus sign.
I stare at the page.
This problem can't be mine—
I cannot solve it!
It does not make sense.
Now my head is hurting,
And my shoulders are tense.
"Lord, help me," I pray,
Then hear Him say,
In a whisper to my heart,
"Make a start,
Do your best,
And the rest
Will work out all right."
I know it will,
Only through God's might!
The answer might be wrong,
But I'll know I tried,
And that gives me pride.

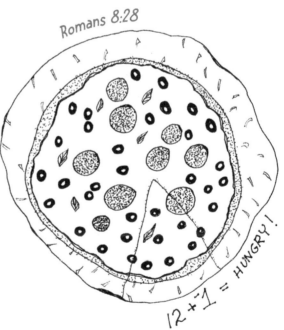

Romans 8:28

12 + 1 = HUNGRY!

Proverbs 18:4

ENGLISH PAPERS

They say it's essential to write
Right!
To try hard, with all your might.
To scribble
Without quibble
The story you're telling,
And don't forget the spelling.
'Cause your mom needs flour
From the store,
But your teacher wants flowers
At her door.
I can't take it anymore!
I'm absolutely frustrated—
My lonesome sole soul
Will ne'er again be whole
Unless English papers can be dictated.
(Siri? Alexa? Are you listening?)

HOMEROOM

I just heard words of doom and gloom—
My two best friends have a different homeroom
Than me.
It can't be!
We've been with each other since second grade.
Everything we've done, all we've made,
Has been together.
We sold lemonade on our front sidewalk,
Spent overnights in frivolous talk,
Together!
I don't want this school year to start.
I need a Band-Aid on my heart.

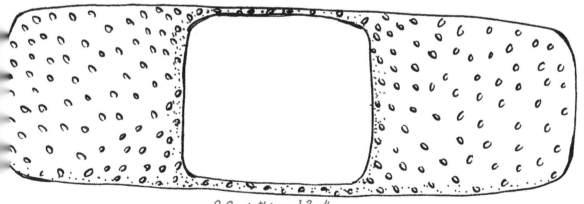

2 Corinthians 1:3—4

A TEACHER'S LIFE

My teacher
Can be annoying
When he says we should be enjoying
The privilege of learning.
Doesn't he know we're yearning
To go outside and run?
He must hate to have fun.
While teaching complex science,
His smile cannot be real.
Does he know how his students feel?
He must have a perfect life,
One with no pain or strife,
Because his resolve never fails
When every student wails
For mercy and a break from homework!
Then at the store on Saturday,
I see my teacher and hear Mother say,
"Is there any way we can help you?
You need five hands and have only two!"
My teacher carries a crying child
While two other small ones run wild
Through the store.
It must be a chore to keep up!
"Thank you," he says as she takes the baby.

"I thought I could do this, but maybe
I do need an assist.
Since my wife broke her wrist
And can't drive,
I can barely keep us alive!"
I'll remember this in class
And take a pass for a while on complaining.

Galatians 6:2

1 Timothy 6:6–10

CONTENT

There once was a pig who thought he could fly.

He couldn't. Oh my!

Then there was a dog who wished she was a frog,

But she couldn't croak. No joke!

If all of God's creatures

Loved each of their features,

We all would be glad.

None would be sad

With the world a more peaceful place.

Living with hearts full of grace,

We could each find the space

To grow

And show

Each other love.

TO AVOID SINKING

Shivering alone by the side of the pool,
I think it unjust and terribly cruel
That I must relearn what I knew once before.
As an unborn baby, I could float free and glide
Through the warm waters of my mother, inside—
I could swim!
Now watching my friends jump in and cheer,
I follow so they don't see my fear—
I sink.
Reaching the bottom, opening my eyes,
I watch air bubbles float toward the skies
And remember to push up.
Flexing my knees, thrusting my feet,
I burst out of water into air that is sweet
And breathe.
What other things have I forgotten?
When I was a babe, swaddled in cotton,
Was there an angel by my crib each night?
If I am struggling alone one difficult day,
I should think it foolish I've not stopped to pray,
Because God has been there from my start.
He created my heart.
And I think,
With Him, I won't sink.
If I remember.

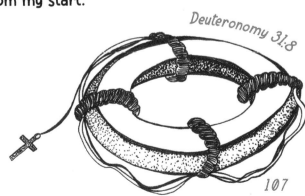

Deuteronomy 31:8

GRANNY'S GARDEN

My granny lives in a magical place
Where gray-green moss drapes the trees in lace.
The garden grows lush behind her tiny home,
Where flowers bloom and children roam.
She says the plants need laughter
To grow happily ever after.
In spring the blossoms are purple and yellow,
Watered each week by a neighborhood fellow
Who has dark slanted eyes
That seem very wise
And four small children with shiny black hair
Who follow Granny and me everywhere.
The children giggle loudly
And Granny says proudly,
"Happiness makes my garden grow,

Mark 12:31

108

For that, I am thankful! Don't you know?"
In summer her yard fills with pink, white, and green.
A sprinkler arcs rainbows—an enchanting scene!
Two tall brothers with chocolate-brown skin,
Come for vacation; we hold hands and spin.
Around in a circle, we laugh and we sing
Until we fall to the ground, breaking our ring.
In the quiet of autumn while kids attend school,
Orange lilies and mums bloom through the cool.
The garden and Granny patiently wait
For winter to come, then something great,
When all of the colors stand together
Joyfully, despite the cold weather.
The holly bush glistens dark green and red.
Visiting children gather 'round with hats on their heads.
The sweaters and mittens, the kind faces too,
Create a wondrous, breathtaking hue
As orange patterns huddle next to the reds
    and the browns,
And they sing of dear baby Jesus in
    Bethlehem town.
Granny says, "This is the garden God loves best,
When all of His children know they are blessed
And show their joy with blossoming smiles
That fill up the earth for miles and miles.
All colors together as one."

FENCE WALKING

I liked walking alone on the top edge of a fence
Until I took a fall that made my mom wince
And tell me not to do it any longer.
But my desire to be up there is much stronger
Than common sense allows!
So I asked my older brother
To tell our worried mother
That he would walk below.
She can trust him; I know,
Because he never fails to protect me!
He may tickle me and tease,
Make me say, "Pretty please,"
But he will always catch me when I tumble.
That's love.

1 Corinthians 13

ANGST

What does it mean
To be a teen?
Is it incredible or sad?
Shouldn't I be glad
To leave childhood behind?
I can get a job and learn to drive a car.
I can leave home to discover things afar.
Meeting new people sounds super fun,
But I'm not sure I'll like every single one.
What if I get lonely?
God created us to be like Adam and Eve,
Stronger together as we work and achieve
Success during our earthly life,
As a team of husband and wife.
Thinking about this is stressful,
So I guess I should stop and pray
For God to show me the way
One step at a time.

Ecclesiastes 4:9–12

MASTERPIECES

Could you hold a pine cone?
Look at its shape; notice the way it has grown
From a new green pod, closed and soft,
Into a dry brown cone whose seeds fly aloft.
All work done when each seed gone;
It's your geometric treasure, so precisely drawn.

Could you fit a seashell inside the palm of your hand?
Pick it up and wipe off all the speckles of sand.
Study the intricate patterns and lines
Like an artist had painted them as signs.
See that He is right there in front of your eyes;
Take this shell home as a valuable prize.

Could you catch a feather floating in the air?
Stroke the soft vanes, light as tiny hairs.
Admire how they're connected firmly to the shaft,
Engineered exactly to catch an upward draft.
Tuck this feather in your hair
Or in a buttonhole to wear.

Ponder these masterpieces.
Are they merely pretty things
Or miraculous works by our Creator King?

Psalm 19:1

One protects beginnings of new majestic trees;
The next offers haven to creatures in the seas.
One gives earthbound life a way to reach the sky,
To climb toward the heavens, to soar, to fly.
And, most amazing, they are all works of art—
Beauty to nurture our longing hearts.

So when you next try to make anything,
Be filled with happiness, work, laugh, and sing.
Because you too are meant to create,
Created yourself by a God who is great!
    You are a masterpiece.

HATEFUL WORDS

Hateful words lie.
They hold no truth.
And that is why
You should NEVER believe them!

Jeremiah 7:8; Proverbs 12:22

BETWEEN THE NOW AND NOT YET

This is a concept that's hard to get:
What lies between the now and not yet?
Why are there hard things in life?
Adults may argue about this question.
For some it becomes a sad obsession,
Leading to anger at God.
Yet each child knows the answer
    within their heart,
Babies too, because they are smart
And remember their heavenly Father.
We know there cannot be dark without light,
Wrong without right,
Or sweet without sour.
Even though it's within God's power
To make all things good all of the time,
If God did that, we would lose
The freedom to choose
Love.
If this causes you confusion or pain,
Know surely, with faith in Christ you gain
Eternal joy.

1 Peter 5:10

TRINITY

As a word, it just means three:
Trinity.
Our Creator walks with us as one:
The Father who made us
And Jesus, His Son.
His life for ours, Christ Jesus gave,
So this must change how we live and behave,
Because, for us, death has no power—
We have the Helper from Christ each earthly hour.
The Holy Spirit guides us on earth 'til our graves,
Staying close beside all who are saved.
The Trinity,
Three in One,
Intended salvation for everyone.

1 Corinthians 8:6

John 14:26

RHYTHM

Silence, then sound: weak, strong,
Boom, tat-tat, short and long,
These noises make a rhythm.
Ordered, recurrent, again, again,
The drumbeat, then a violin.
Soon there is a symphony.
The conductor stands in front and leads,
Noticing problems, meeting needs
For guidance.
Outside a thunderous, boom, boom, crack:
Drops hit the ground, smack, smack,
As it rains.
Rivers fill, giving water to drink.
Wilted flowers lift in sync
As a life sonata pours from above.
Raindrops stop, frogs rumble gruff,
An owl whispers whoo-whoo with a puff
Of cleansed night air.
Turtledoves coo, a mockingbird sings,
Then God lifts His hand and brings
A new morning's concert.
Inside each waking person, a heart is beating,
Lub-dub, lub-dub, repeating, repeating,

Through what the day brings.
A rush to get ready, heartbeat speeding,
Breakfast, backpack, a book for reading
In quiet moments.
For years and years, the days pass by.
People laugh together, sometimes cry
As they navigate life.
Ordered, recurrent, again, again,
This rhythm stops and then
A person's world-song ends.
Death comes to each person living on earth.
It follows sometime after their birth,
But only when our Lord allows.
God, our conductor, is mighty and wise.
He is with the baby born, with the old lady who dies,
Because they are His children.
The rhythm of life, the timing of death
Lies with the one who gives us our breath,
Who has lovingly made our forever home,
Where everyone makes beautiful music!

John 5:24; Ecclesiastes 12:7

THE GREATEST

Inscribe these words upon your heart.
Say them out loud as your day starts.
"FAITH, HOPE, LOVE!"
Place them firmly in your brain,
Since God says they will always remain.
"FAITH, HOPE, LOVE!"
In a world so imperfect it's hard to see
Living examples of all three,
Pray for the superpower to be
These invisible things.
And with the greatest, perfect love,
God will give you this joyful ability from above!
Have faith, have hope—
He's sending a huge LOVE delivery so you can cope
With all the wondrous adventures that lie ahead!

1 Corinthians 13

FAITH   LOVE
HOPE

If I speak in the tongues of men or of angels, but do not have love,
I am only a resounding gong or a clanging cymbal. If I have the gift of
prophecy and can fathom all mysteries and all knowledge, and if I have a
faith that can move mountains, but do not have love, I am nothing.
If I give all I possess to the poor and give over my body to hardship
that I may boast, but do not have love, I gain nothing.
Love is patient, love is kind. It does not envy, it does not boast, it is not
proud. It does not dishonor others, it is not self-seeking, it is not easily
angered, it keeps no record of wrongs. Love does not delight in evil but
rejoices with the truth. It always protects, always trusts, always hopes,
always perseveres.
Love never fails. But where there are prophecies, they will cease;
where there are tongues, they will be stilled; where there is knowledge,
it will pass away. For we know in part and we prophesy in part,
but when completeness comes, what is in part disappears.
When I was a child, I talked like a child, I thought like a child,
I reasoned like a child. When I became a man, I put the ways of childhood
behind me. For now we see only a reflection as in a mirror;
then we shall see face to face. Now I know in part; then I shall know fully,
even as I am fully known. And now these three remain:
faith, hope and love. But the greatest of these is love.

(1 Corinthians 13)

For God so loved the world that he gave his one and only Son,
that whoever believes in him shall not perish but have eternal life.
For God did not send his Son into the world to condemn the world,
but to save the world through him.

(John 3:16-17)

ORDER INFORMATION

Additional copies of this book can be ordered
wherever Christian books are sold.

Printed in the USA
CPSIA information can be obtained
at www.ICGtesting.com
CBHW062225301124
18111CB00003B/3